# vegetables coloring book

**F. FRANKLIN**

# Testing page

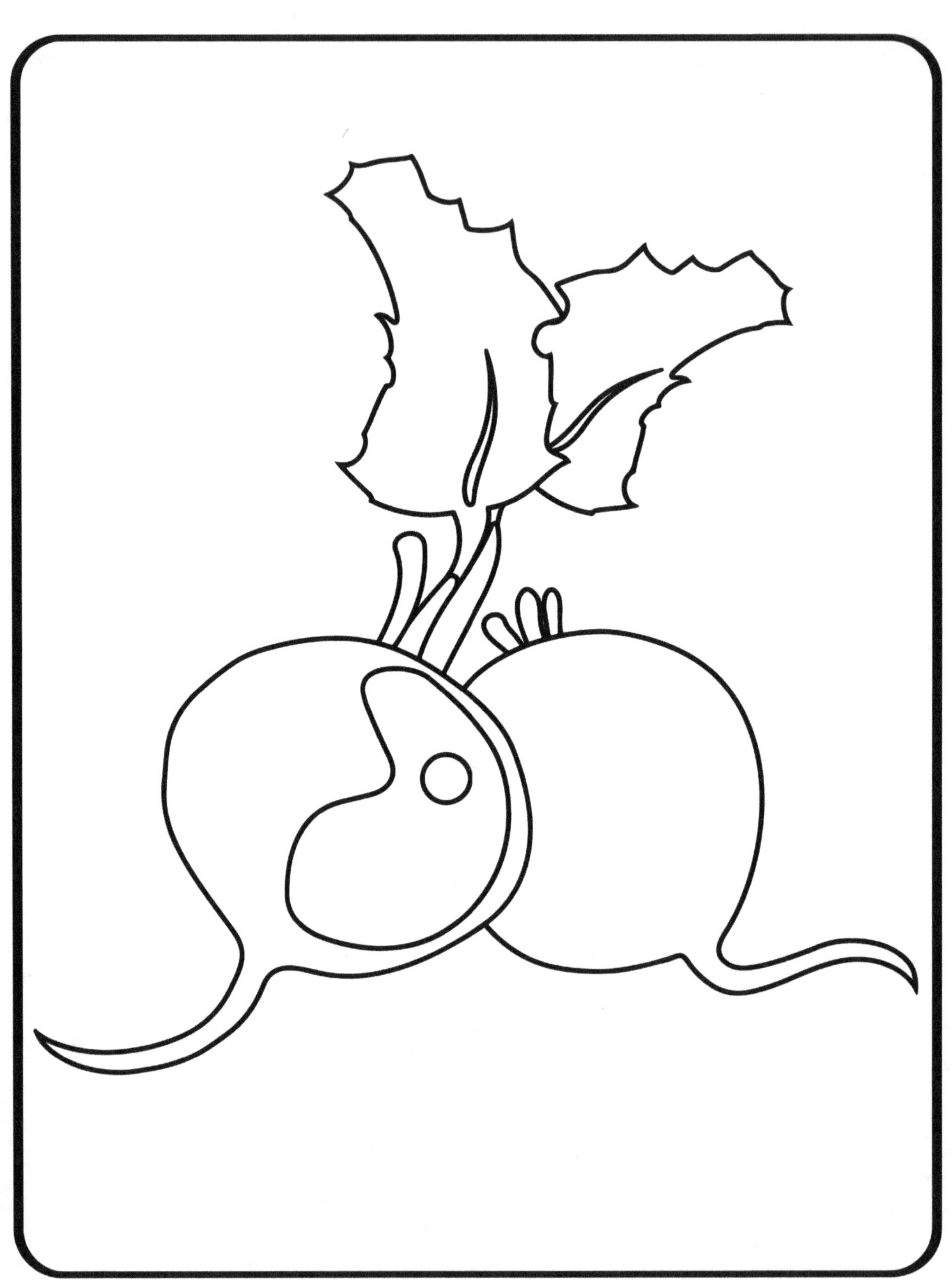

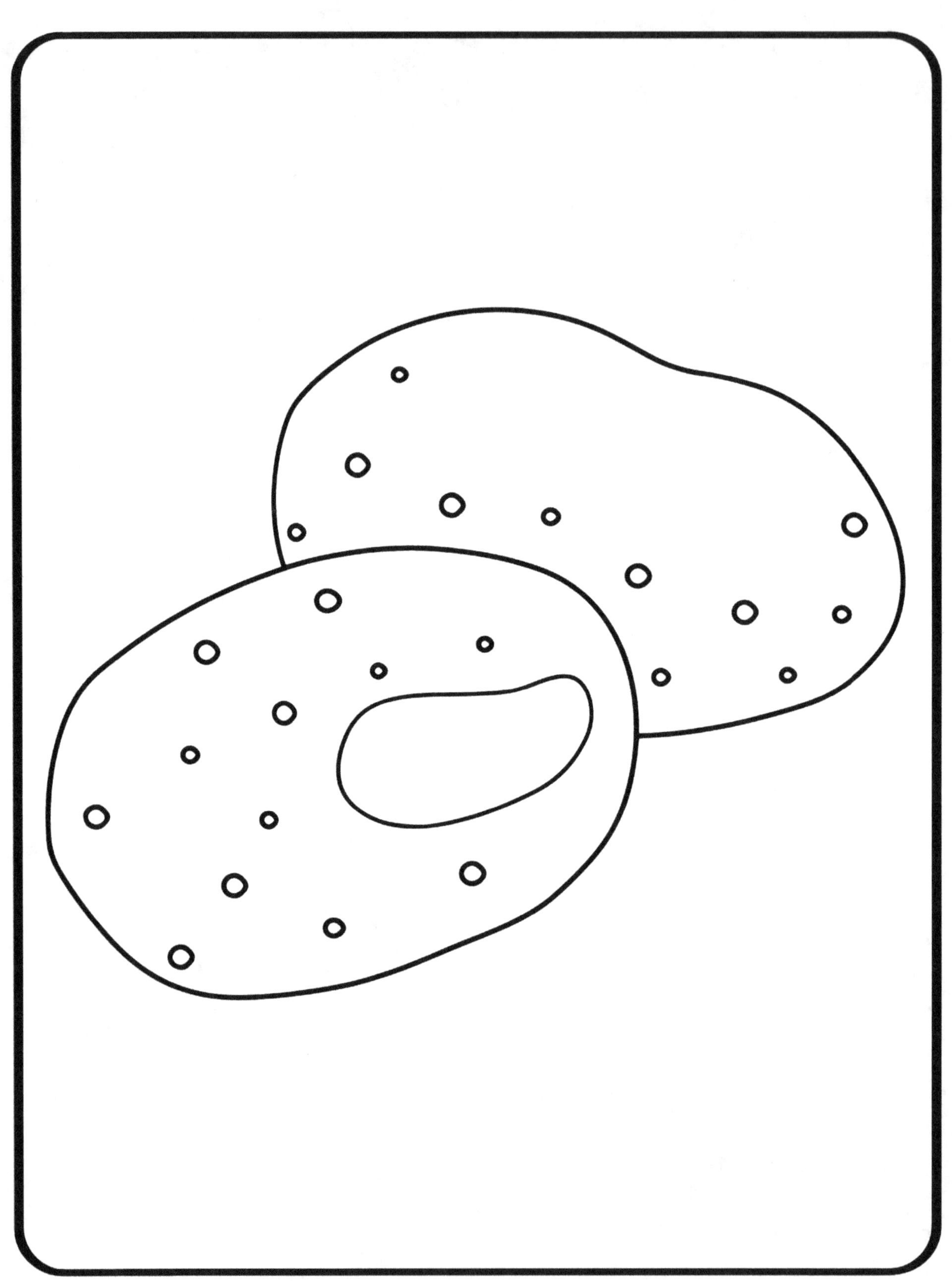

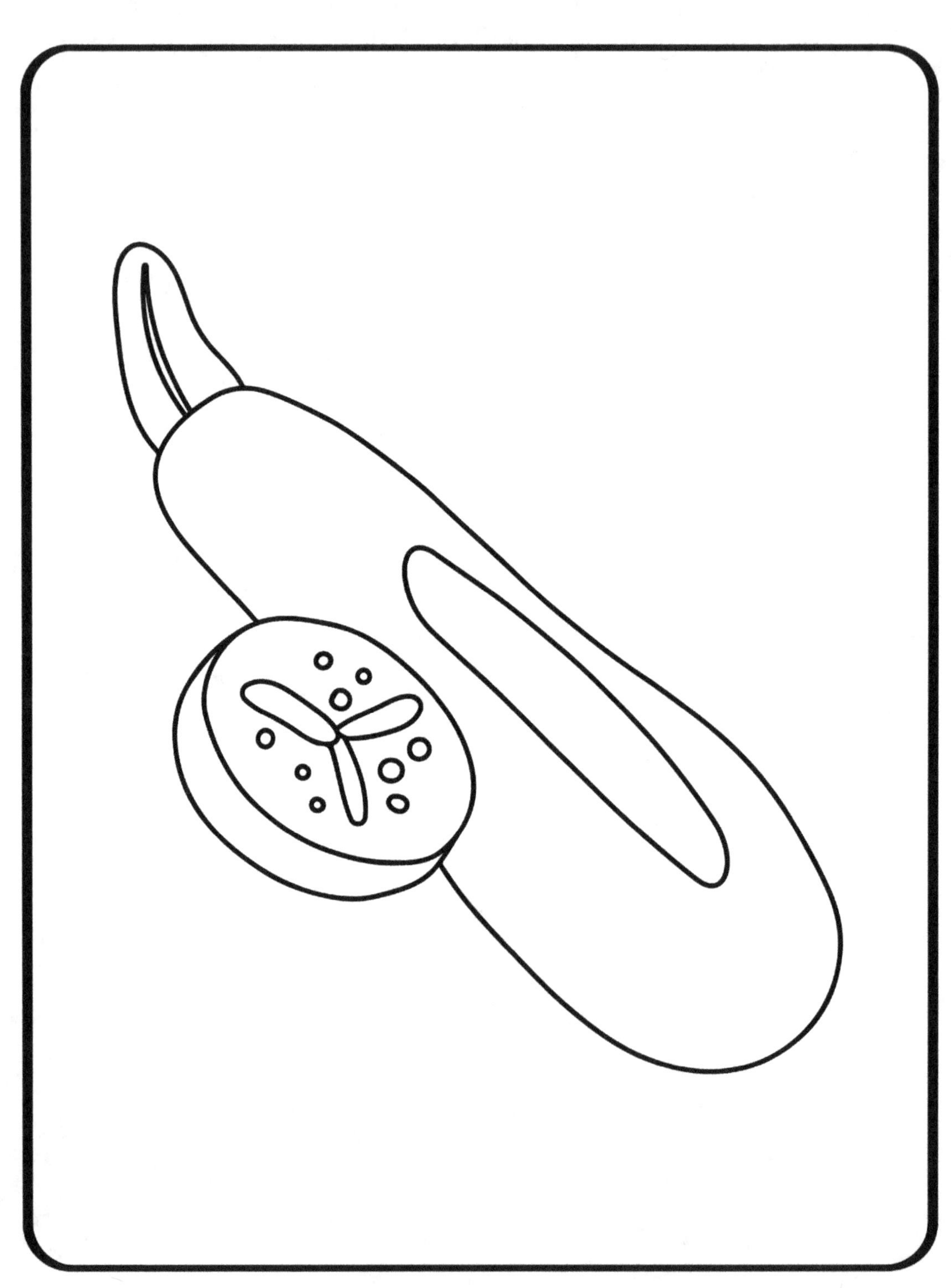

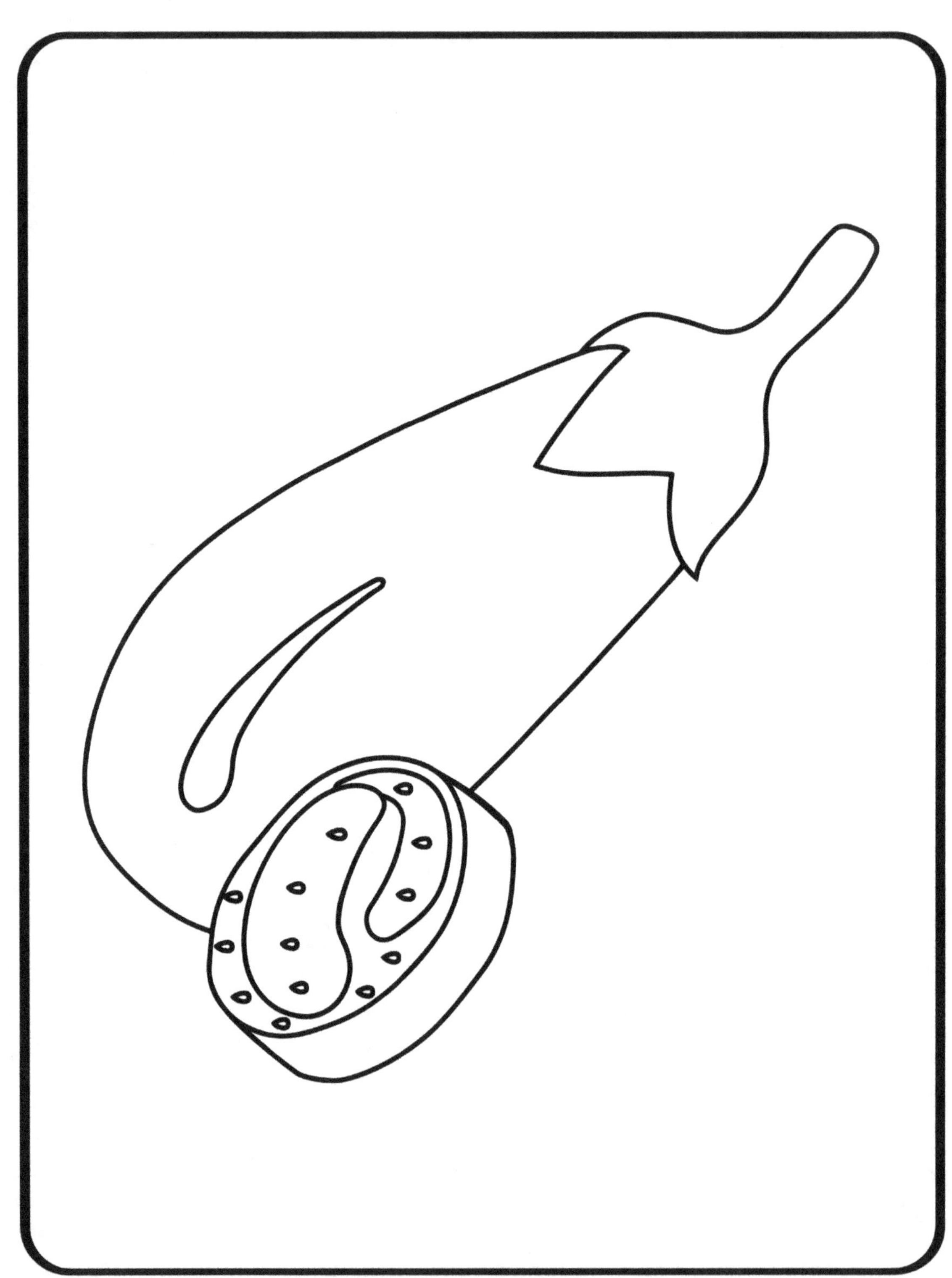

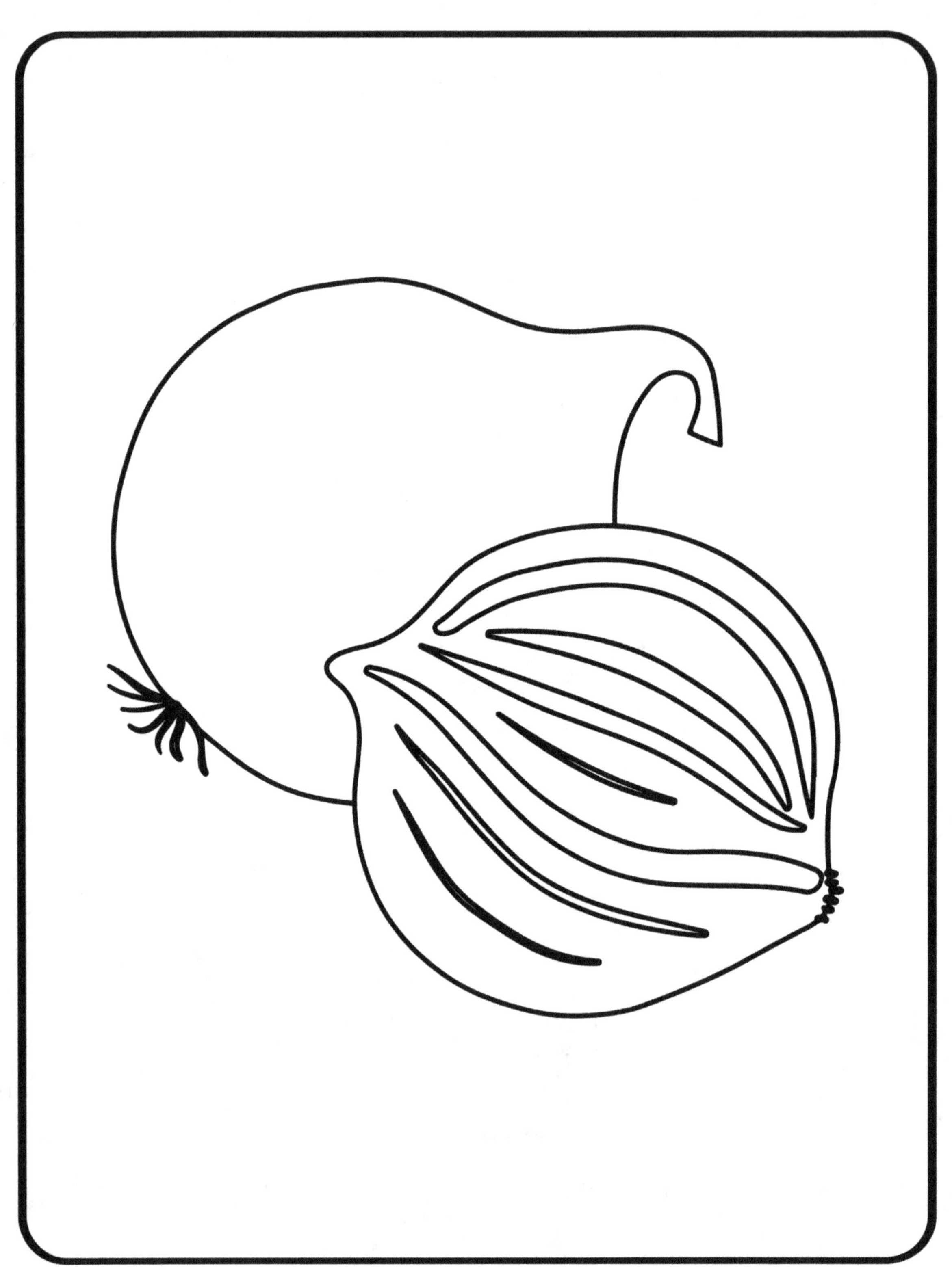

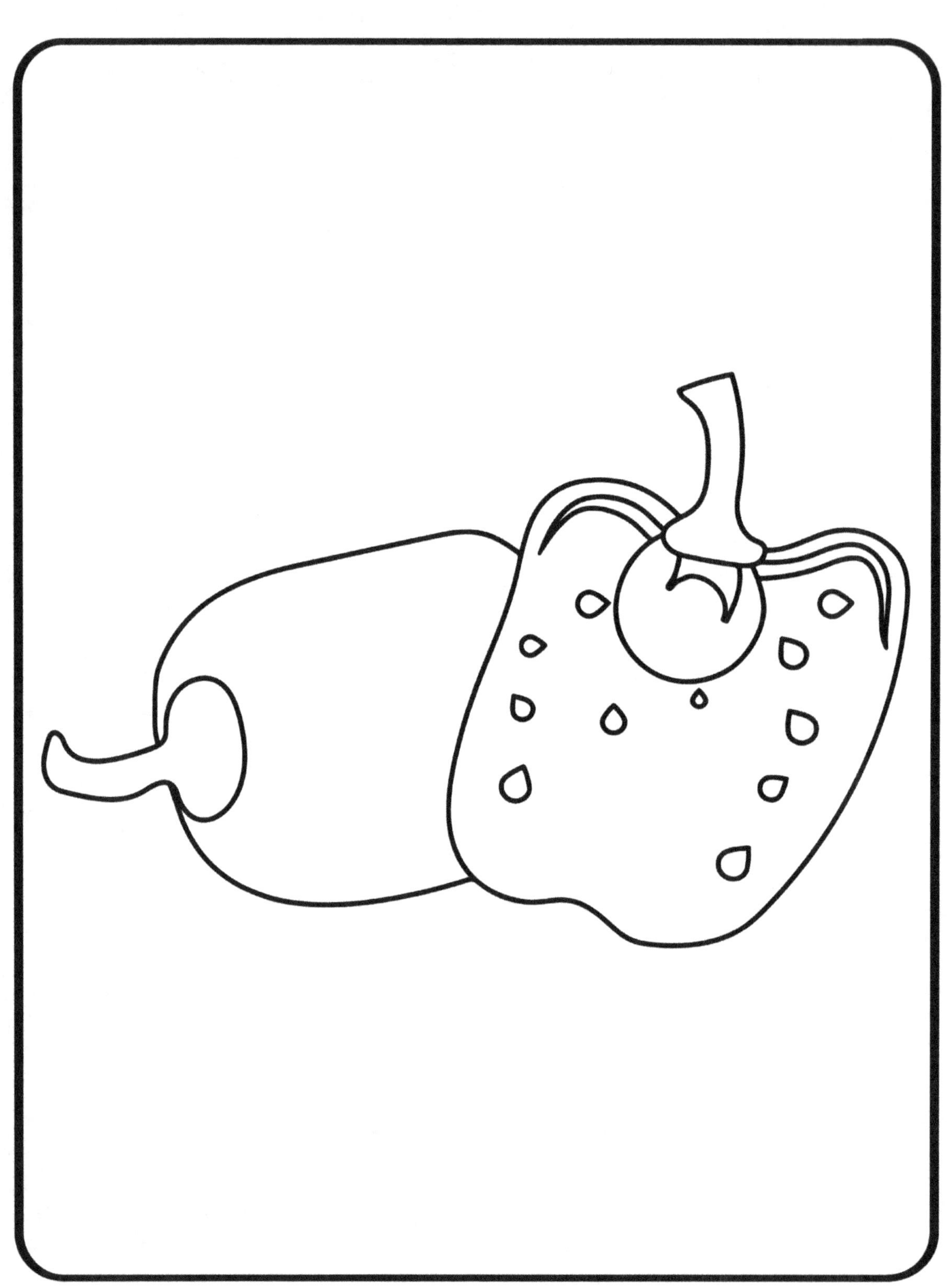

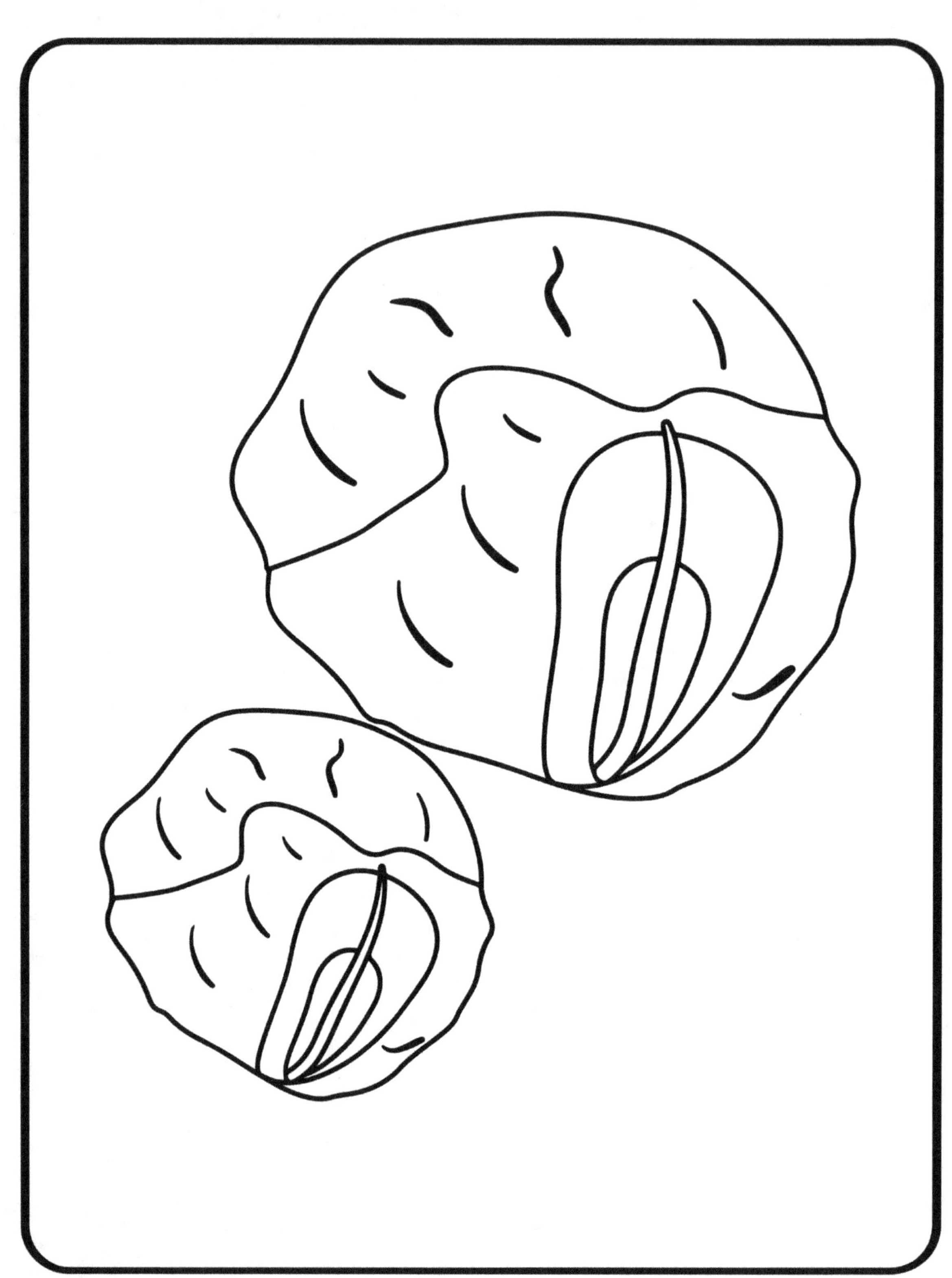

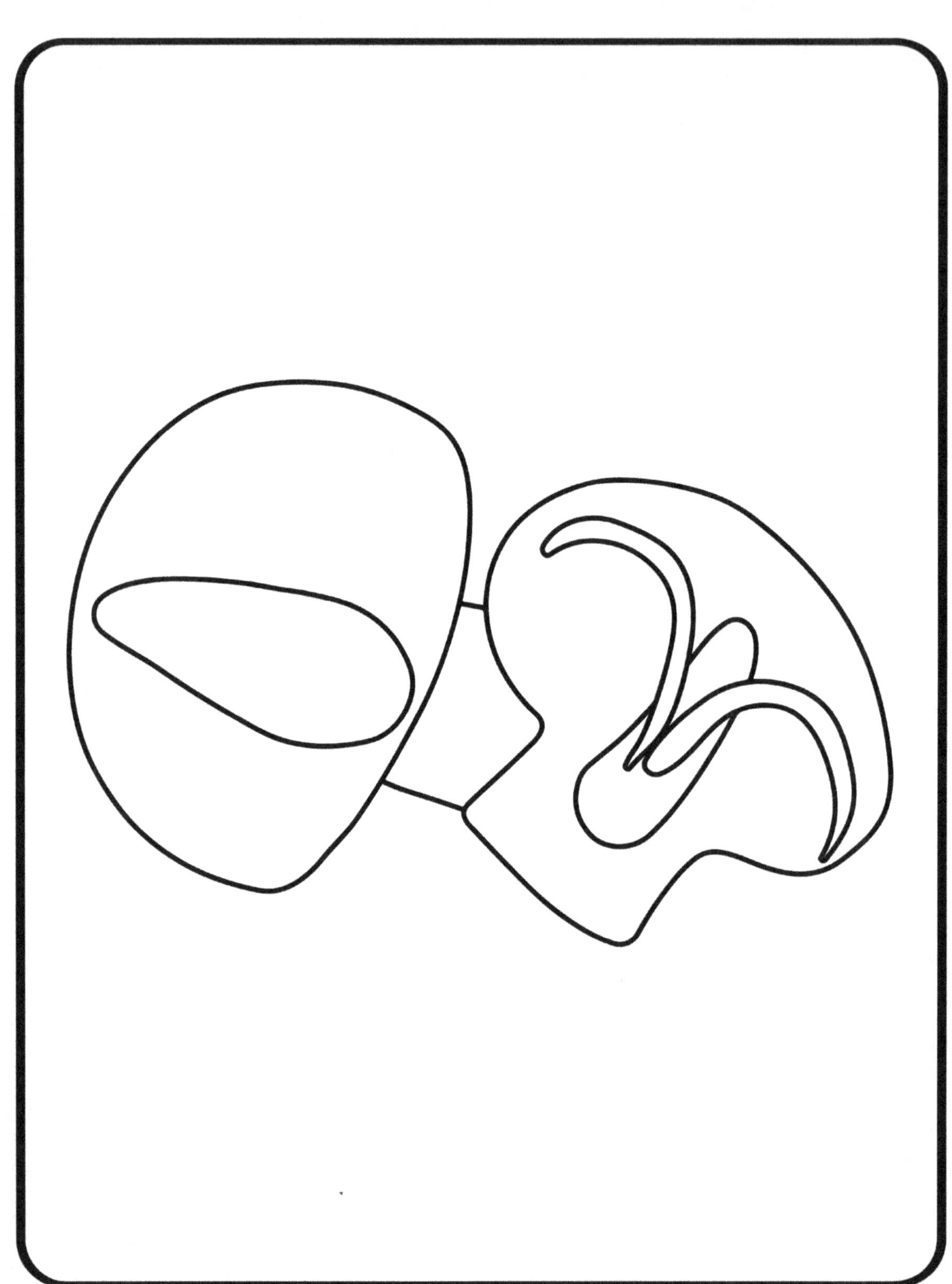

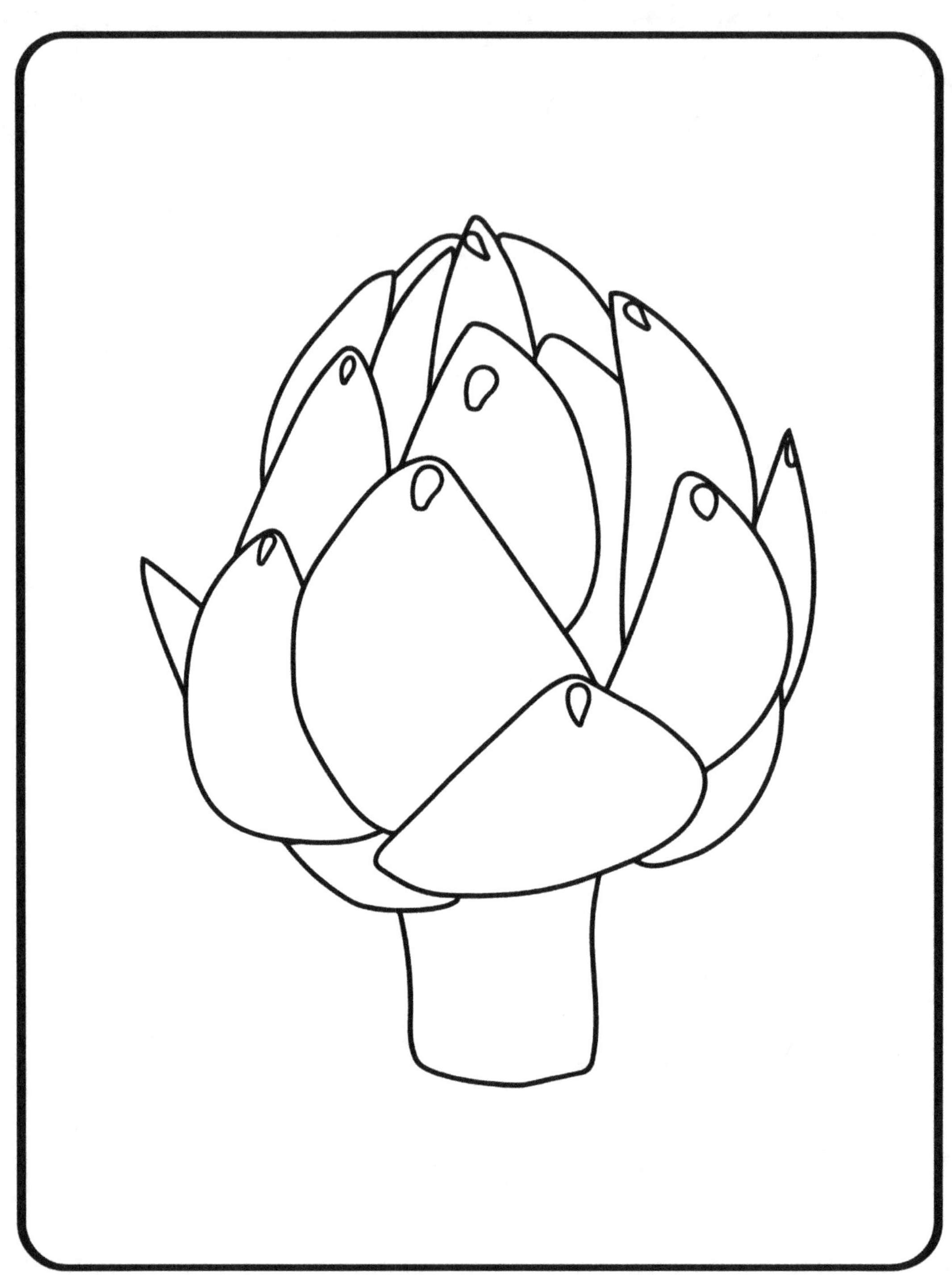

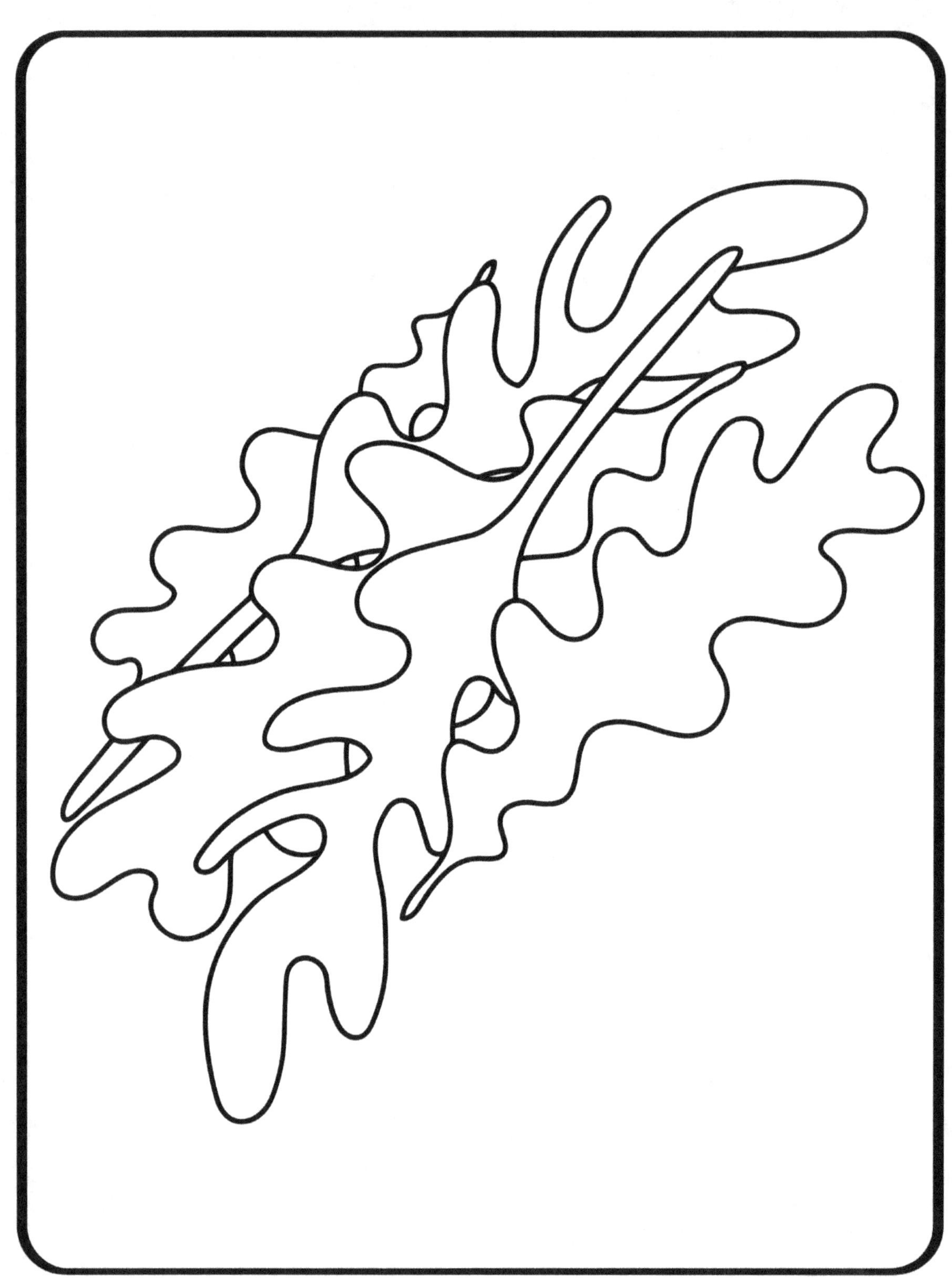

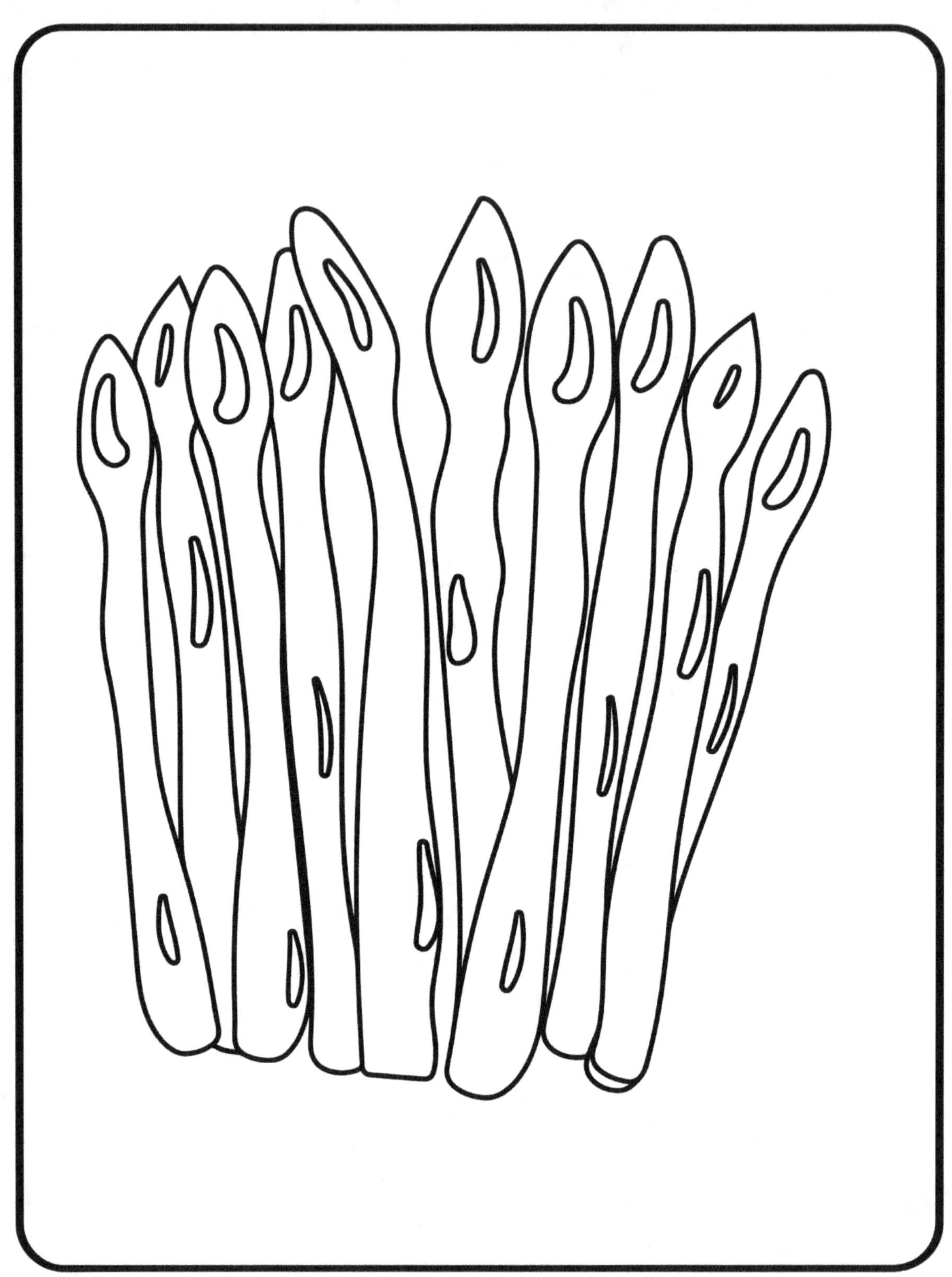

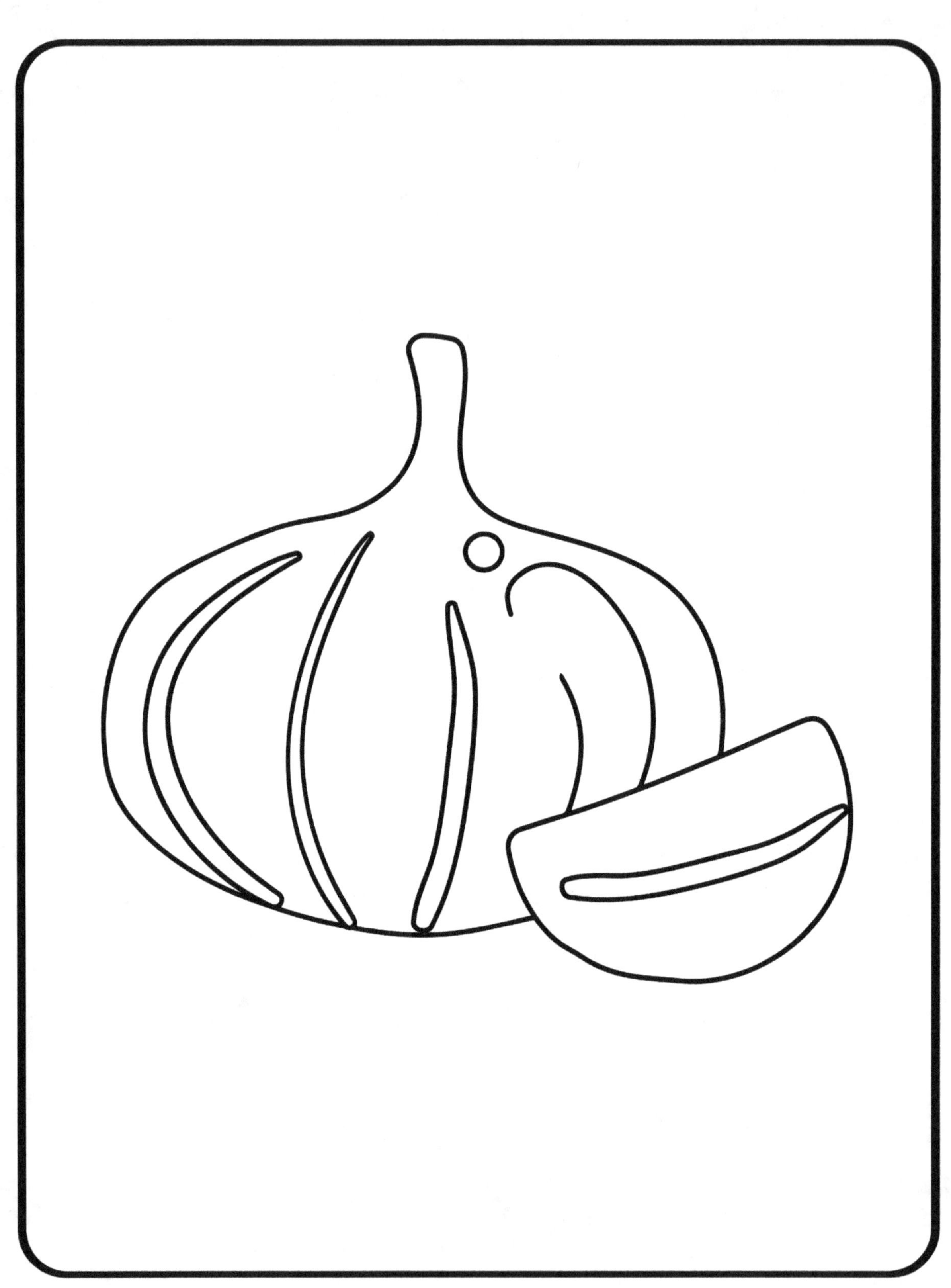

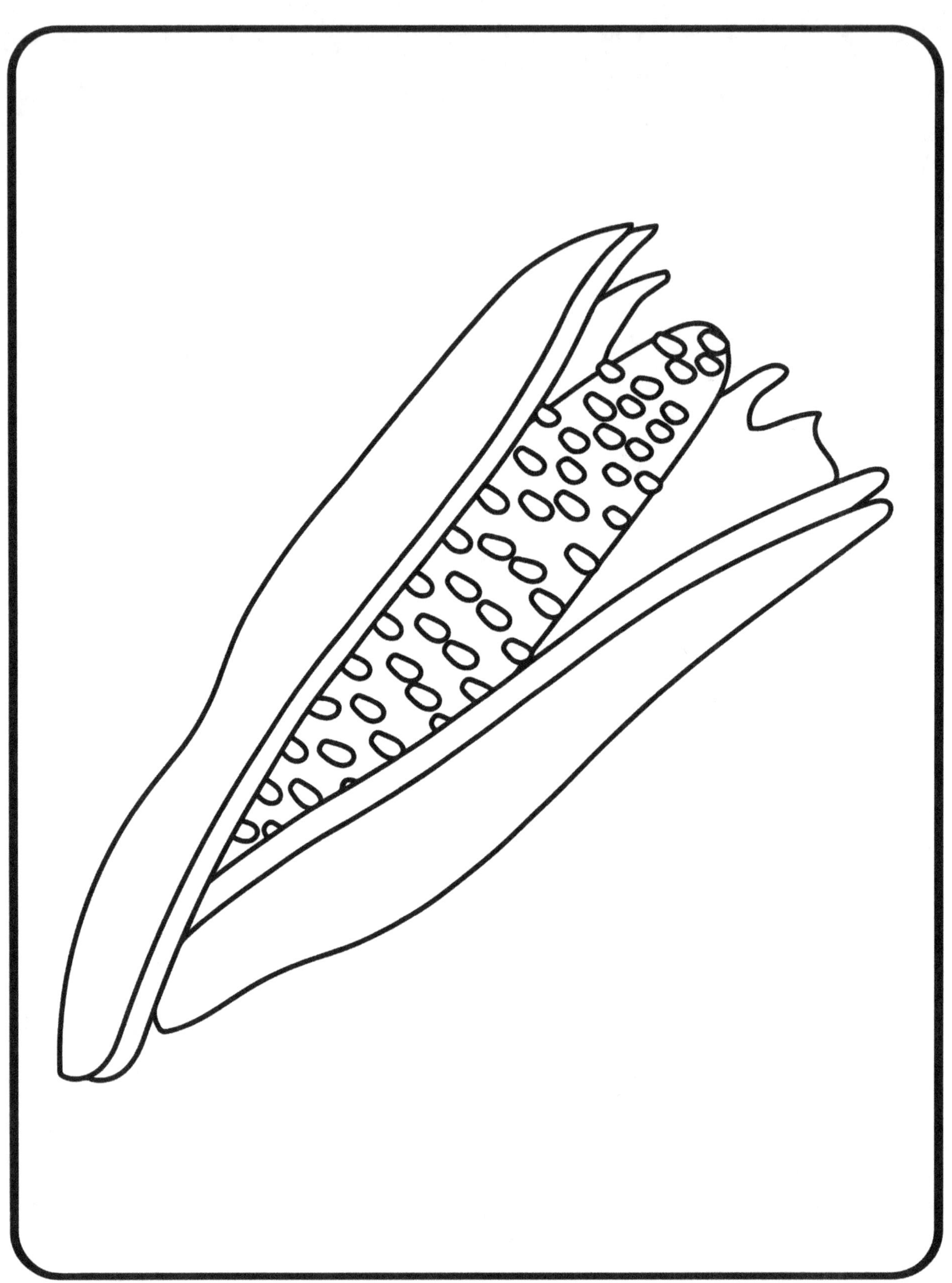

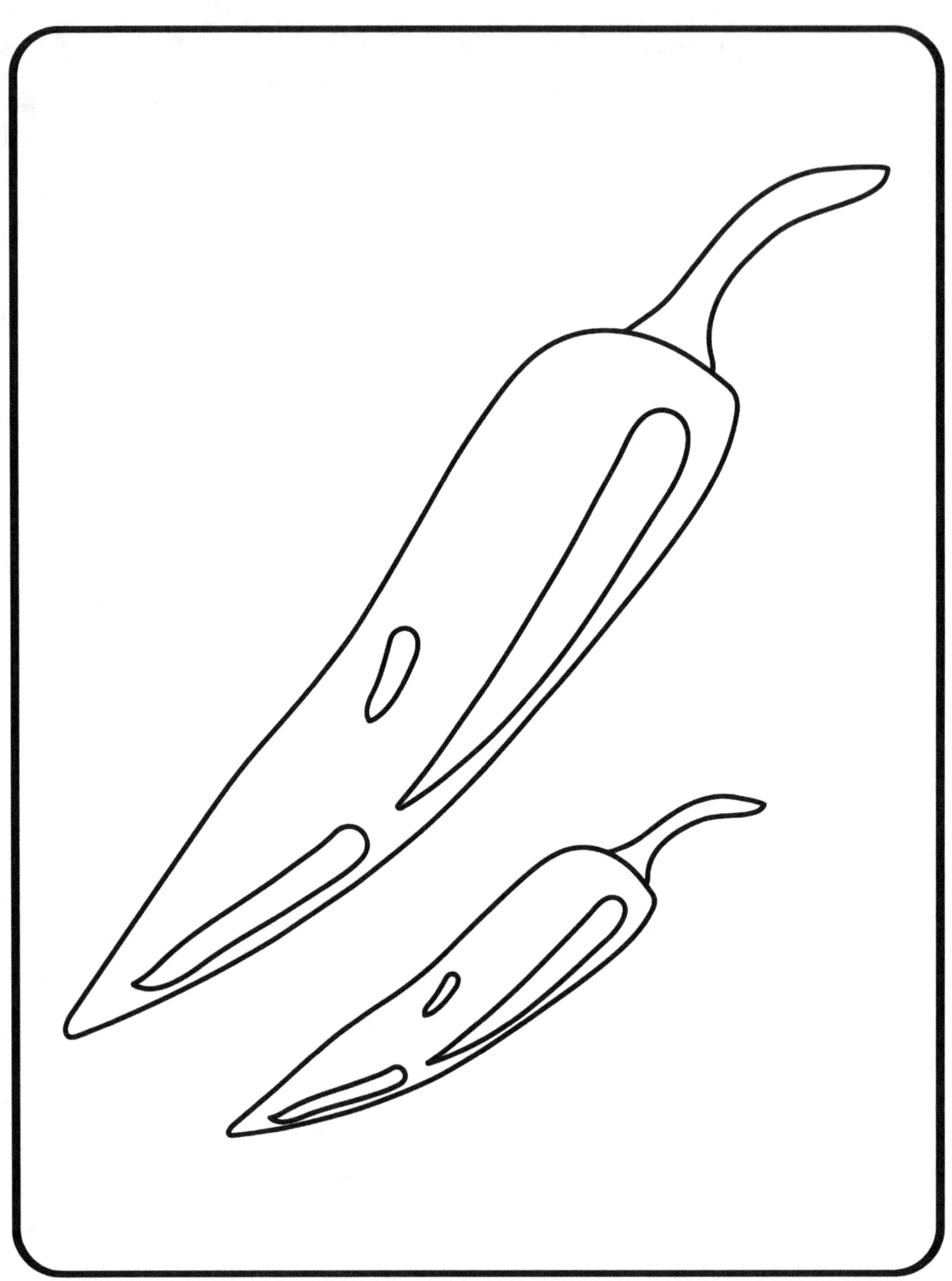

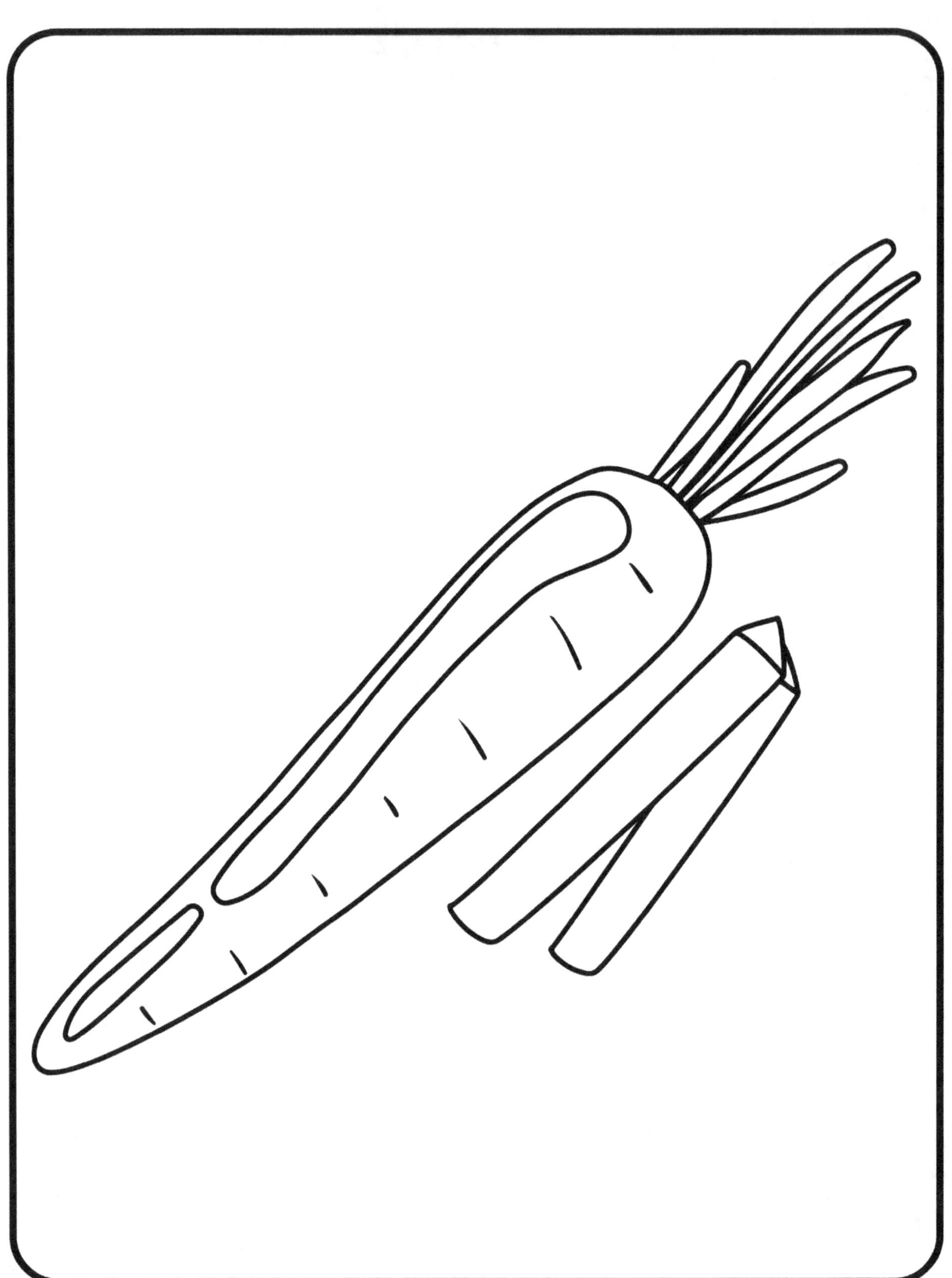

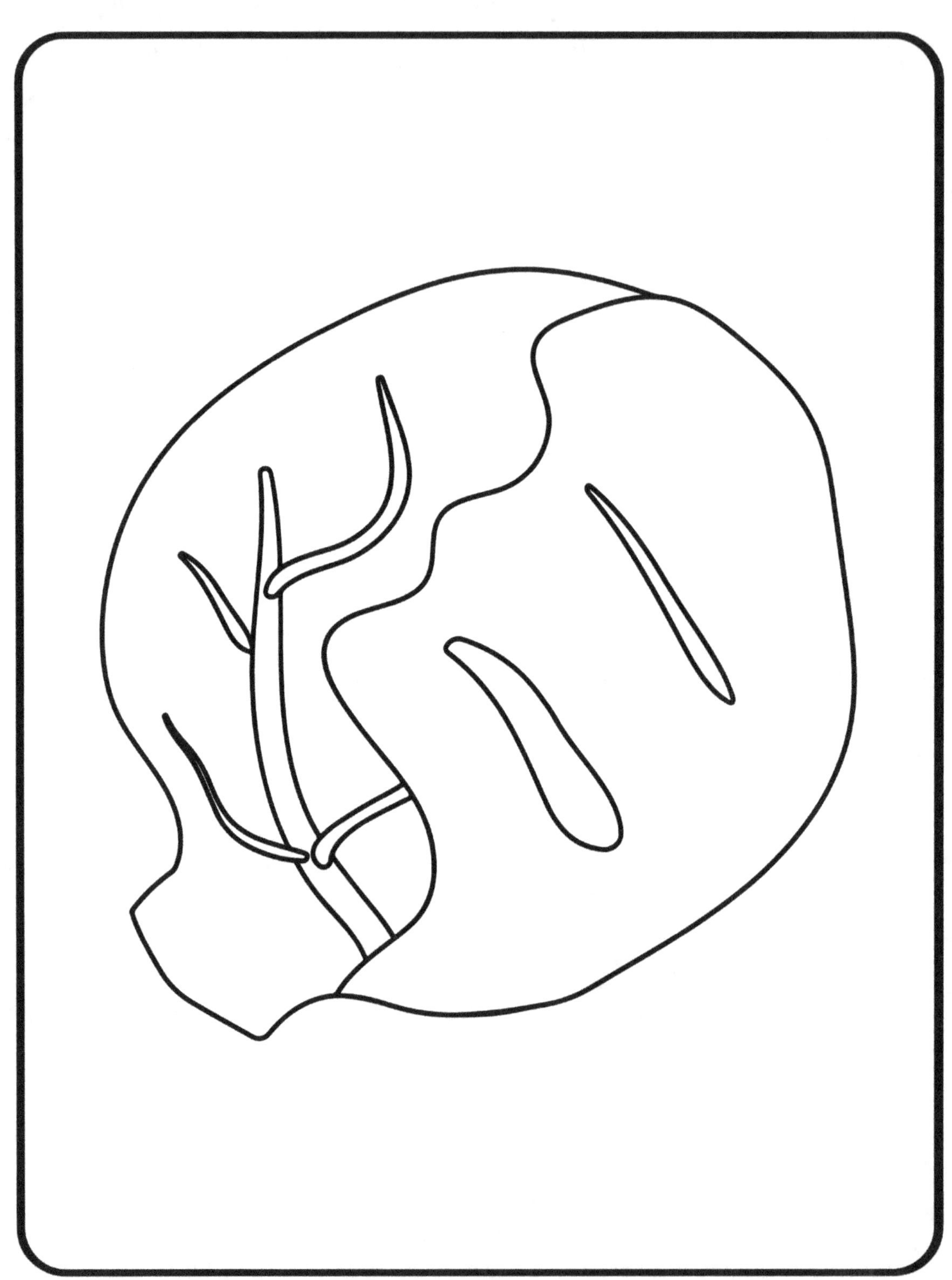

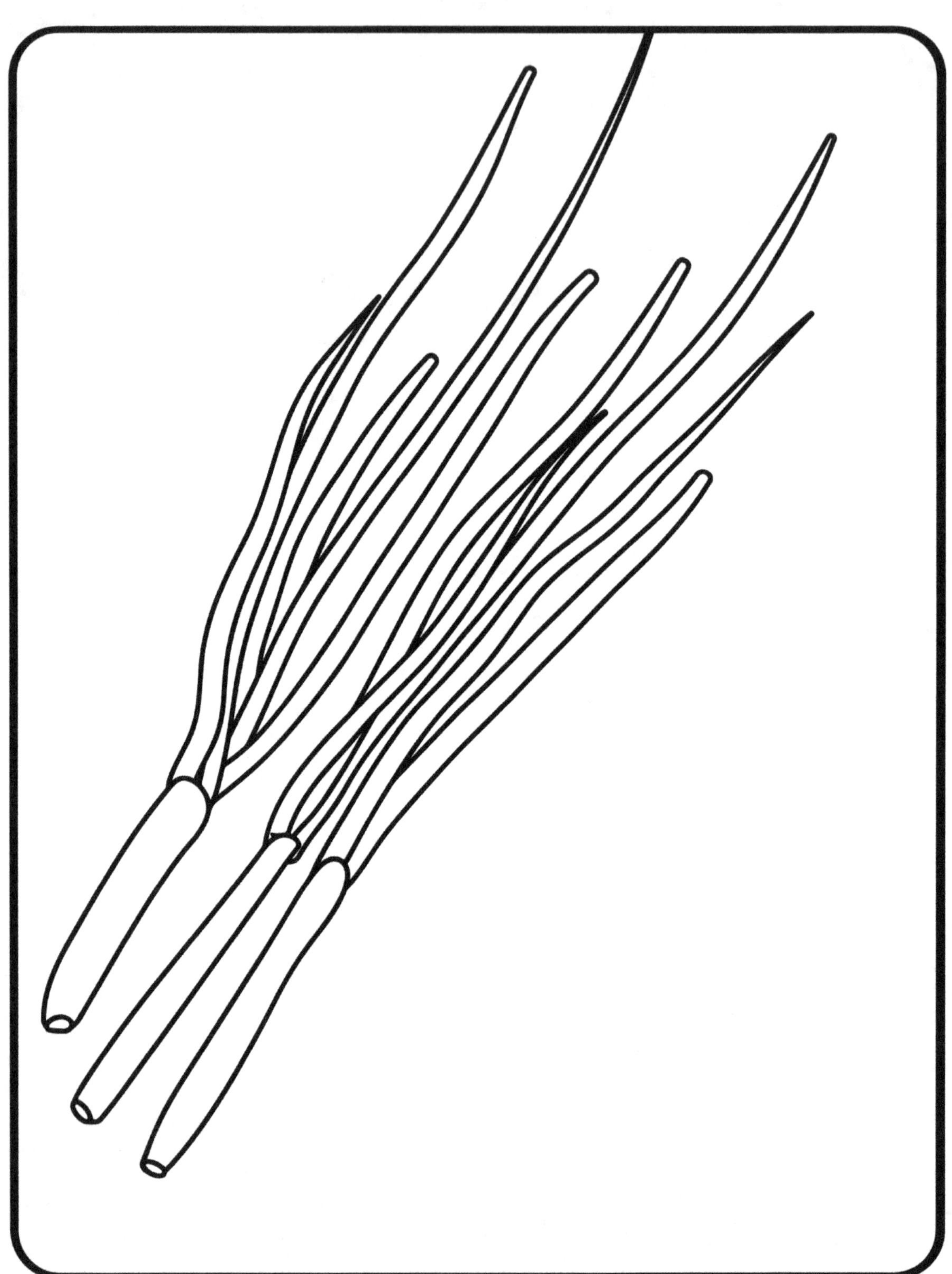

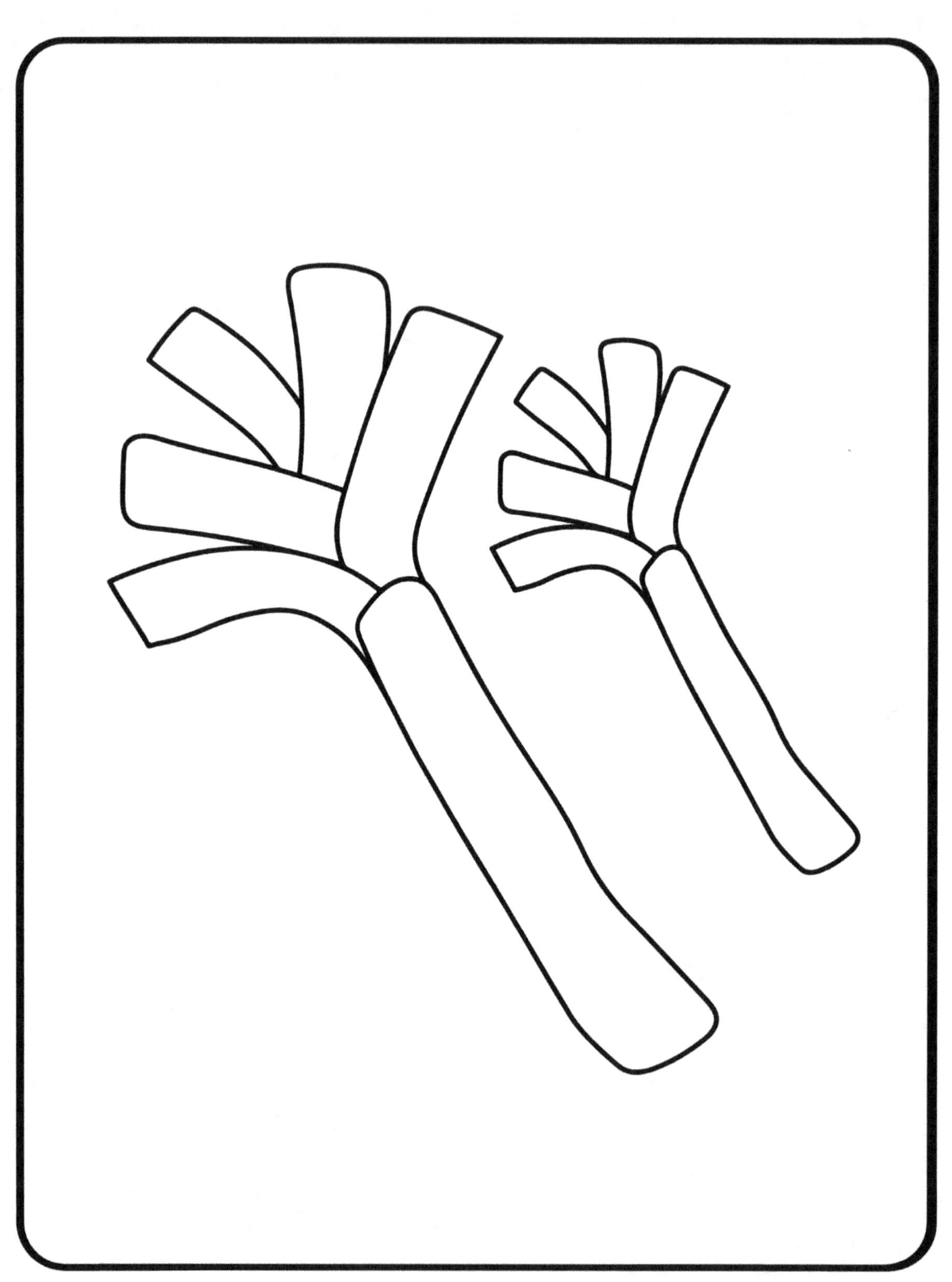

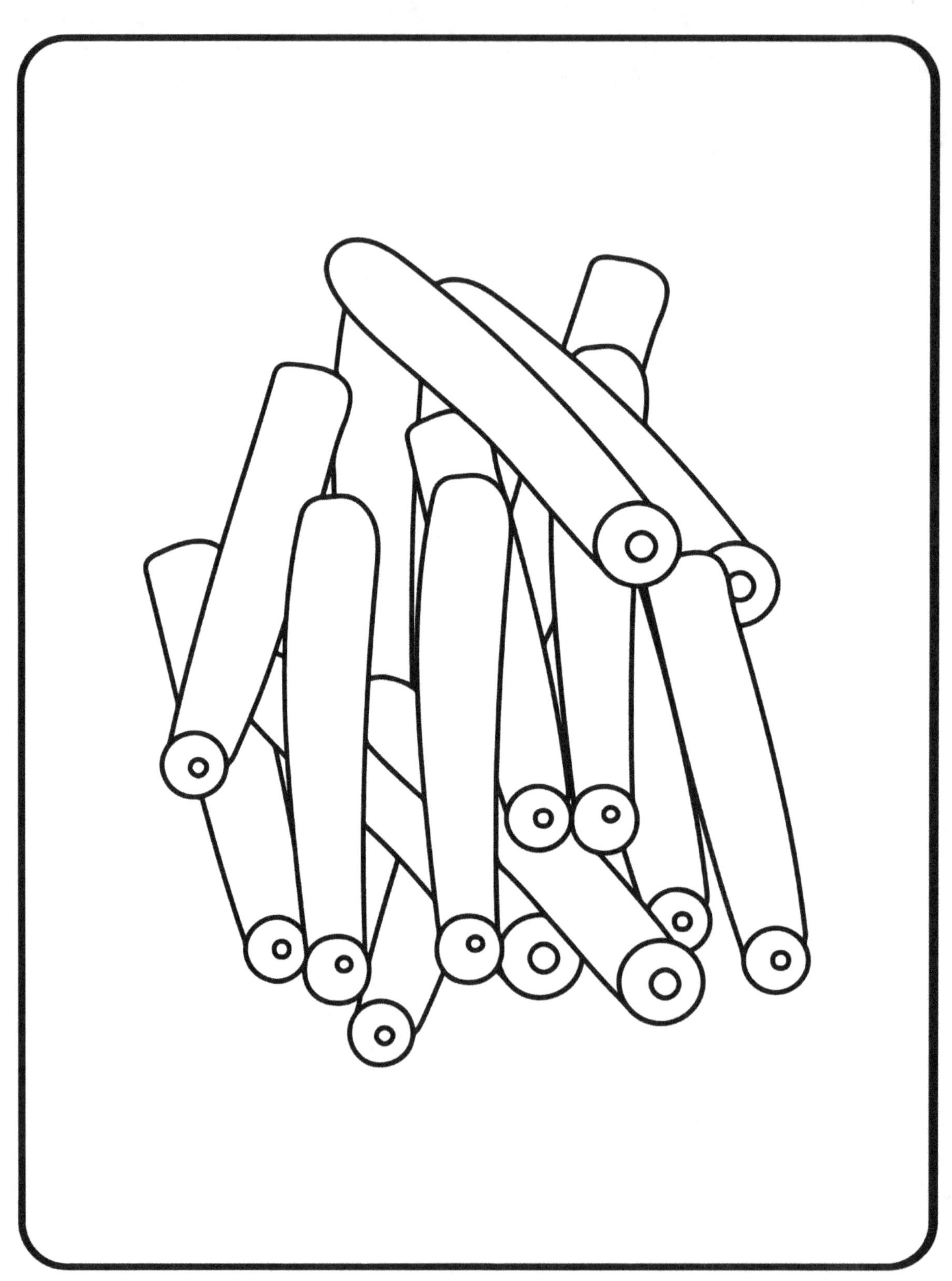

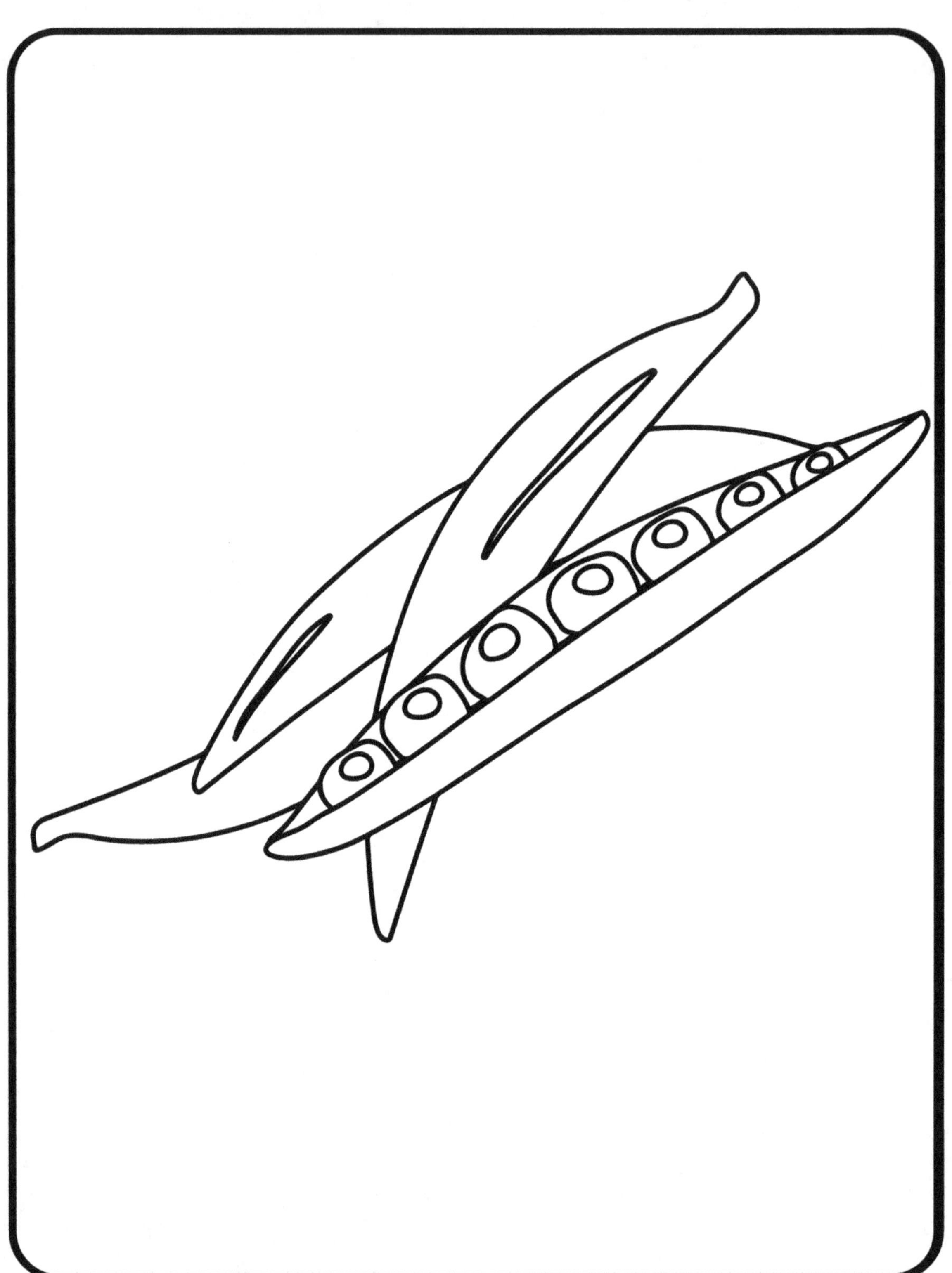

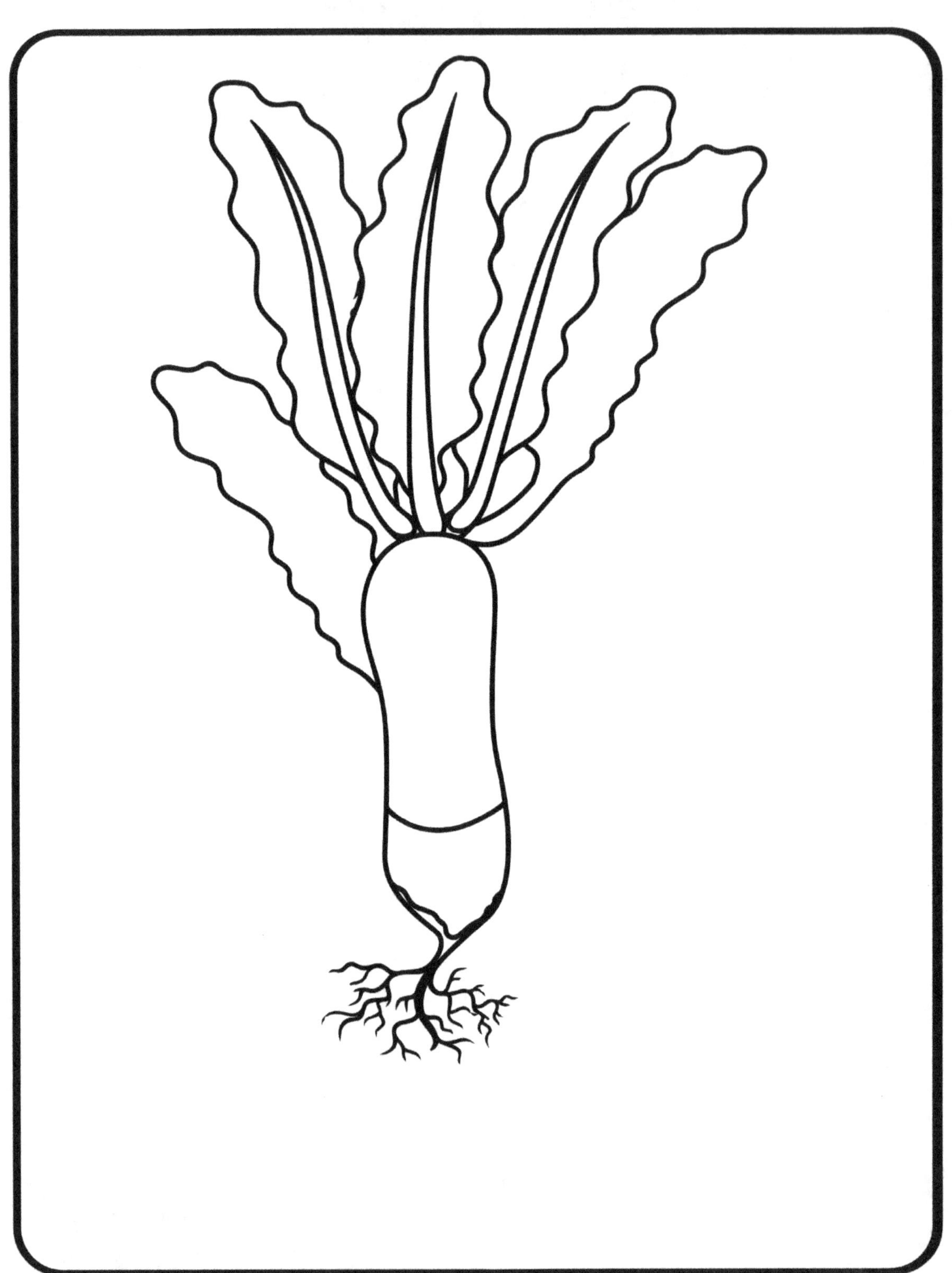

www.ingramcontent.com/pod-product-compliance
Lightning Source LLC
Chambersburg PA
CBHW081454250726
48662CB00009B/3087